CONTENTS

FEAST AND FUN

What is a festival?

Did you have any special celebrations with your family last year? Perhaps your birthday was one of them. Were there others? Did you eat special foods, sing, dance, or play games? Did you have a bonfire, wear a costume, or join a parade?

A birthday is a small festival. It is often celebrated just by the family and close friends. In some places, however, everyone who was born in the same year celebrates their birthday on the same day. This is a much bigger festival. It is a festive occasion for the whole community to enjoy. The Chinese people celebrate everyone's birthday on their New Year festival.

A festival is a feast day, a time for merriment and celebration. People need to have time to enjoy themselves, to have a change from work and school. They also like a good feast. So they have their festivals, just as you do. Some people's only holidays are when they celebrate their festivals.

Often the whole community celebrates together, as in this midsummer festival in Sweden.

6

FESTIVALS

Beverley Birch

Macdonald Educational

How to use this book

First, look at the contents page opposite. Read the chapter list to see if it includes the subject you want. The list tells you what each page is about. You can then find the page with the information you need.

If you want to know about one particular thing, look it up in the index on page 31. For example, if you want to know about Passover, the index tells you that there is something about it on page 25. The index also lists the pictures in the book.

When you read this book, you will find some unusual words. The glossary on page 30 explains what they mean.

Series Editor
Margaret Conroy

Book Editor
Peter Harrison

Production
Susan Mead

Picture Research
Diana Morris

Factual Adviser
Sheena Crawford

Reading Consultant
Amy Gibbs
Inner London Education Authority
Centre for Language in Primary
Education

Series Design
Robert Mathias/Anne Isseyegh

Book Design
Julia Osorno/Anne Isseyegh

Teacher Panel
Steve Harley
Anne Merriman
Jenny Mules

Illustrations
Lorraine Calaora 6-7,14-15,20,28-29
Julia Osorno 18,26-27
Maggie Raynor 10-11, 12-13, 16-17,
24-25

Photographs
Cover: Children celebrate in Brazil
Barnaby's Picture Library: 19 (Kraus),
23
Nick Birch: 8
Camera Press: 13 (Western Way), 14
(Spaak), 21 (Moore), 25 (Praun)
Werner Forman Archive: 17
W. MacQuitty: 7, 29
Anne & Bury Peerless: 22
Homer Sykes: 9, 27

Families often enjoy a special festival meal, as in this Chinese home at New Year.

How festivals develop

Many of our festivals remind us of a story or event. The event may have been important in the history of our country, or the festival might celebrate a legend or the changing seasons.

The festival of the Lilies in the Italian town of Nola is 1600 years old. People used to dance holding lilies on poles. The 'lilies' are now huge steeples. Each steeple is built and carried by a different group of workers in the town.

All over the world people mark these kinds of occasions with festivities. They celebrate the good things in their lives, and ask for success in the future. People became afraid that the Sun would disappear during the winter. They held bonfire festivals to honour the Sun and ask for its safe return. Now, not everyone believes that the Sun will disappear, but people in many countries still have fire festivals to cheer up the dark winter days. They make winter seem less cold and gloomy.

Many of today's festivals began a long time ago, and are a mixture of customs and beliefs from different people through the ages.

For example, Hallowe'en is a blend of three very old festivals. One is the ancient Celtic New Year bonfire festival to the sun god, when people believed that the souls of the wicked took on animal bodies. The second is the Roman festival to Pomona, goddess of fruit, when people used nuts and apples in the games. The third festival is the Christian one of All Hallows, when people remember the dead. Which of the different festivals do Hallowe'en costumes and masks, games and stories of ghosts come from?

A model of a Viking ship is burned during the fire festival of Up-Helly-Aa in the Shetland Islands, far off the north coast of Scotland.

Custom and tradition

Every festival has its own foods and customs, clothes, music, dances, plays or decorations. Many of the customs are very ancient. They remind people of the story behind the festival.

Homes all over the world are bright with candles during winter festivities. For thousands of years people have used candles to remind them of the light of the Sun and of new life in the earth after winter. They use candles as special signs, or symbols, of these things.

At festivals we also often eat special foods as a symbol. In harvest celebrations, for example, people usually prepare foods from the newly-harvested crop, like the sweet rice cakes eaten in the harvest festivals in India. Mince pies are an ancient Christmas food in Britain. They are a symbol of the wise men's gifts to the new-born Jesus, and the pies were once made in the shape of Jesus' manger.

Christmas evergreen trees are a symbol of life continuing after the darkness of winter.

Festival customs come from many different peoples in history. Some Christmas customs were once part of the winter festivals of ancient non-Christian peoples. Early Christians chose the date because at this time Romans celebrated their two festivals, Saturnalia and 'the Birthday of the Unconquered Sun'.

The Yule log, candles, and evergreen leaves are traditions from the Viking Yule festival. The traditional Christmas pudding, ball-shaped and carried to the table in flames, was once a symbol of the Sun.

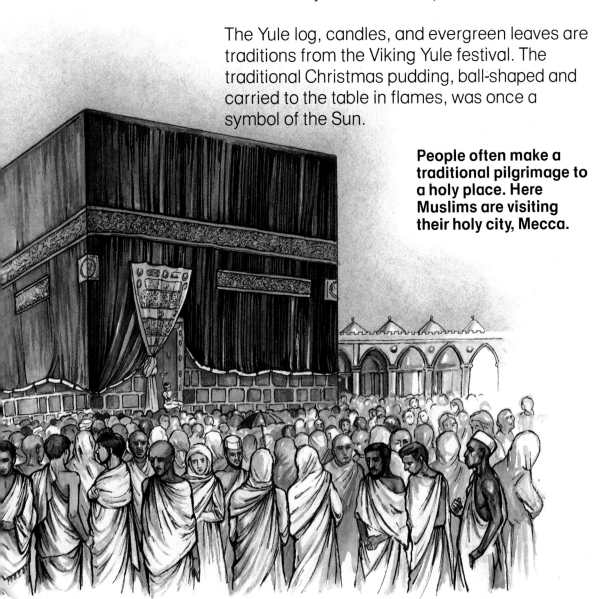

People often make a traditional pilgrimage to a holy place. Here Muslims are visiting their holy city, Mecca.

LIFE AND NATURE

Celebrating life

Can you imagine what it would be like to have floods which ruin the harvest? Or storms which make it dangerous to go to sea just when the fishing season is about to begin? Or no rain for months, so that no crops can grow? Times like these are frightening, for without food we die.

We survive by using the Earth's soils, seas, its rivers, lakes, weather and changing seasons. We can grow crops, keep animals, hunt for fish or animals, and find materials for clothing, tools and shelter. So when storms ruin our crops, or there is no rain to help plants grow, our struggle to survive is much harder.

Many festivals began because people wanted to ask their gods for success in finding food and other things they needed to survive. Others began because they wanted to give thanks and have a holiday when work was over.

People still celebrate the world of nature like this. Farming people celebrate harvests. Fishing people wish their fishermen luck at the start of the fishing season. City people often celebrate the summer warmth by festival competitions between workers. They hold football matches, horse, cycle or running races, for example.

In the ancient Inca festival of Inti Raymi, Peruvians light bonfires to the Sun, and honour the Christian saint, John the Baptist, by bathing in streams and rivers.

A deer dance performed in the spring in New Mexico, USA. One dance may ask the spirit of the deer for rain, and another for a good hunt.

New life in the earth

Many festivals take place when the Earth seems bursting with new life in the spring. Crops grow and animals breed. People want to celebrate this and the new warmth and light after the dark cold of winter. They ask for fine weather for planting seeds and for a good growing season.

Some countries do not have winter and spring, but wet and dry seasons. There, these kinds of festivals take place after the wet seasons, when people sow or plant new crops.

Once people saw the seasons as a battle between good and evil. When good wins, it is spring. Good reigns through the summer, but is overcome by evil in the winter. Then good must be given new strength so that spring can return. Many spring festivals celebrate this struggle.

Spring in England is a time for Morris dancing. Once this dance was meant to show people pretending to do battle.

Hindus in India celebrating Holi. During the festival, many people visit friends, give each other gifts, and spray each other with coloured dyes.

The Hindu festival of Holi is one of these. People burn an image of the legendary demon Holika as a symbol that good has defeated evil. They burn rubbish, to show that past wrong doing is forgiven. They offer some of the winter barley harvest as an offering of thanks to the fire, and they eat roast barley.

Some religious festivals are held in the spring. These use symbols which are really reminders of new life in the earth at this season. The traditional Easter egg means new life. The egg is a very ancient symbol. It was used long before the Christian festival of Easter began.

15

Harvesting

When people have gathered in the ripe crops, they hold festivals. They want to give thanks for the harvest. They need a holiday after the work. Harvest is often a time of plenty, when people can enjoy the foods they have grown or look forward to the money they will earn when they sell their crops.

Some people think that the spirit of life itself lives in the crops. They believe that if they cut the crop, they kill this spirit of life. So they have ceremonies to make sure that the spirit will be reborn and give life to the seeds planted for the next year.

In harvest festivals all over the world, people do this even when they no longer have these beliefs. They make a doll from the last stalks of the crop so that the spirit of the crop can stay in the doll. In a festival in Lithuania, people dress the last sheaf of grain with ribbons and flowers, so that it looks like an old woman. They keep this 'boba' (old woman) until the next year.

There are often ceremonies of the first tasting of the new crop. In one rice festival in India people get up before dawn to boil the new rice. They watch eagerly, and as the first bubble rises in the pot, they cry 'Pongal! Pongal!' — a signal that the festival has begun. Later they eat a sweet made from new rice, sugar, fruits and butter.

The Christian Festival of the Trays, in Portugal. People carry trays laden with bread to church.

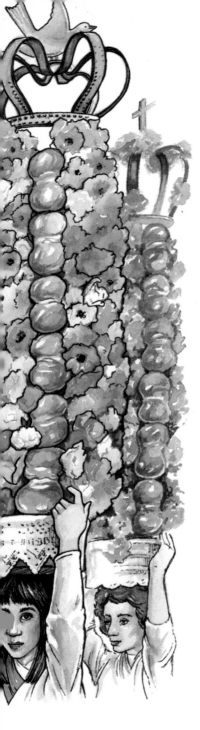

In many parts of Africa the yam harvest festivals are great celebrations, with joyful processions, dancing, singing and a lot of eating.

In the region around the Swiss city of Zurich, lanterns are made out of turnips after the harvest.

17

New Year good luck

Do you celebrate New Year on January 1, or at some other time of the year? Some people celebrate it in the spring, others in the autumn.

Whatever time of year they have their New Year festival, people say goodbye to the old and welcome the new, and follow customs which they hope will bring good fortune. In some countries they wear new clothes, and clean and decorate their homes specially. Many think of it as a time when they should end quarrels.

In Europe people shout out the old year, and greet the new with church bells, fireworks and even car hooters. They have been doing this since times when they believed that noise would frighten away evil spirits. Austrians think it is unlucky to eat crayfish or lobster at New Year, because these shellfish move backwards, as if into the past.

All over the world people send their family and friends wishes for good fortune in the coming year. The Scots have a very old custom for bringing good luck. A person with dark hair must be the first guest to enter the house after midnight, carrying symbols of food and warmth — bread, salt and coal. The person is given whisky in return. The food and fuel which they carry is a 'promise' that everyone in the house will eat and be warm for the next year.

On Japanese New Year, every child has a new kimono to wear. The whole family visits temples and relatives.

People honour and decorate their cattle during the Indian festival of Bohag Bihu, at New Year.

FAITH AND BELIEF

Celebrating beliefs

There are many different kinds of religion in the world. Whatever people believe, they have festivals to honour their religion and to help them think about their beliefs and strengthen them. Sometimes these festivals also celebrate other things, like the world of nature, for people's beliefs are often closely linked to their own particular way of life.

Australian aborigines believe the world was made by the Ancestors. Each clan or group honours an animal, bird, plant, rock or tree, because the clan's Ancestors took its shape. This dance honours the emu bird.

For example, Hindus believe that God appears on Earth in the shape of many different gods and goddesses such as Siva the destroyer, Vishnu the preserver, Durga the demon slayer, Lakshmi the goddess of wealth, and many others. Each of these has temples built in their honour. Each temple has at least one week-long festival every year, and many of these festivals are also spring, New Year or harvest festivals.

In some religions there is a period before festivals when people do not eat for a while, or do not eat certain kinds of foods. This is called fasting. They believe that they clean out their bodies as well as their thoughts. In some religions people make a pilgrimage to a holy place. Sometimes they make an offering to the god or spirit they are honouring. This can be of food, perhaps of fruit or animals.

The Nigerian Yoruba people believe that the spirits of ancestors called the Egungun influence their lives. In a great festival, people dress up as the Egungun to dance in the streets.

21

Days for honouring

In many religions people honour the founder of the religion with a festival. For example, Muslims celebrate the birthday of Muhammad, and Christians celebrate Jesus Christ's birthday.

For Buddhists, the festival of Vesak is the most important festival of all. They celebrate it on the full moon, in honour of the birth, 'awakening' and death of the Buddha.

Buddha means 'awakened one' — a person who has learned wisdom and understanding of the world. People gave this name to an Indian prince who lived more than 2500 years ago, teaching people to practise a way of life so that they could also become awakened.

There is a kitchen in every Sikh meeting place. Preparing and eating food together is an important part of the religious life of Sikhs.

In different countries Buddhists celebrate Vesak in different ways. In Japan they use spring flowers to make tiny shrines and put models of the Buddha inside. In Sri Lanka people light their homes brightly.

In November, Sikhs celebrate the birthday of Guru Nanak, the founder of their religion. For two days before his birthday, people meet to read from their holy book, the Guru Granth Sahib, continuing day and night until the birthday dawns. During the ceremony, they share a meal made from flour, butter, sugar and water, and everyone eats from the same bowl as a symbol that all Sikhs are equal before God.

Buddhists bath and dress in white for Vesak. On this day they pour oil on lamps to honour the Buddha's teaching.

Strengthening faith

People also hold festivals so that they can put aside time to think about their beliefs and make their faith stronger. They often fast before these kinds of festival, then end the fast with a special feast. These are festivals of merriment to celebrate the religion after the time of solemn thinking and worship is over.

This is what happens at the Muslim fast of Ramadan. Muslims eat and drink nothing from dawn until nightfall each day for a month. Then there is the joyous festival of Id-ul-Fitr. Children wear new clothes, and older members of the family shower them with gifts and pocket money to spend on special treats.

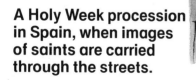

A Holy Week procession in Spain, when images of saints are carried through the streets.

Easter, and Holy Week just before it, are very important for Christians. They remember the death and resurrection of Jesus and all it means to them. In many countries there are huge Holy Week processions. Some Christians fast on Good Friday, the day on which Jesus died.

Passover is an important Jewish festival. Jews celebrate it in memory of the Israelites' flight from Egypt in the time of Moses, and they follow customs to remind them of the story. No leavened foods (foods made with yeast, such as bread) are allowed in the house. In the evening there is a family meal called the Seder, when people eat bread without yeast in memory of the hurried escape from Egypt. There are other symbolic foods as well, such as bitter herbs, to remind them of the misery of slavery.

For Jews, the egg is a symbol of new life. A roasted egg is one of the foods always on the Seder table at Passover.

SPECIAL DAYS

Holidays and fun

People often put aside days simply to enjoy themselves. They may be celebrating an event in the history of their country, as the Americans do at their Thanksgiving. This festival started when the Pilgrim fathers celebrated the first harvest after leaving England and settling in America.

In Scotland people enjoy Burns Night, the birthday of the poet, Robert Burns. They feast on haggis, a sheep's stomach filled with seasoned meats, suet and oatmeal. In Scotland there is also a famous summer Festival of Arts, the Edinburgh Festival. People from all over the world come to enjoy music, dance and plays. The festival lasts for three weeks.

There are arts festivals in many cities in Europe. Sports festivals also occupy the warm summer months. In France, cycle races are often the main events, as well as fairs, picnics, dances, music and plays.

Japanese people mark the flowers coming into season with celebrations such as their cherry blossom and hollyhock festivals in spring. On the children's festival of Hina Matsuri, there is a day of parties, fancy dress and displays of brightly-coloured traditional dolls.

This is the Regatta in the Italian city of Venice. The first regatta was in 1489, when the people welcomed the Queen of Cyprus. Now, boatmen race on the Grand Canal.

The Durham Miners' Gala in England. Workers carry banners, brass bands play, and everyone enjoys a traditional picnic.

Freedom days

Workers all over the world have a special day of their own when they celebrate the fact that workers have joined together to win better working conditions and a better life for themselves and their families. In most countries the workers' day is May Day, but in the USA and Canada it is in September.

In the USSR and China, May Day celebrations are seen as a day of national success. There are huge parades, displays of marching and dancing and sports and athletics events.

Other kinds of festival which are important in some countries are those when people celebrate that they are free to govern themselves — that they are independent. These countries, many of them in Africa, were ruled for a time by other countries like Britain, France or Belgium. Now they celebrate every year to mark the time when they won back control over their own land.

In Kenya, for example, great crowds gather on Freedom Day to enjoy traditional dancing and music, and celebrate freedom from foreign rulers.

Flag Day celebrations on the Caribbean island of Aruba. Although it has its own flag, Aruba still has links with its old ruler, the Netherlands.

Colourful May Day flag displays and parades in the People's Republic of China are a time of joy.

GLOSSARY, BOOKS TO READ

A glossary is a word list. This one explains unusual words that are used in this book.

Ancestors The people whom a person is descended from. They are often also called a person's forefathers.

Celebrations A way of showing that an event is special by doing something particularly enjoyable.

Ceremony An event during which people perform a series of actions publicly and in a solemn way, usually to show that the occasion is an important one.

Community A group of people who live close together, for example in neighbouring streets or in a small village.

Customs The usual way in which people do things.

Fast A time when people do not eat at all, or do not eat certain kinds of food, because it is part of their religious belief.

Gala A fête, or a day of entertainment and happy festivity for people, with concerts and plays.

Holy place A place which people believe belongs to, or where they like to think about, a god, spirit or saint.

Legend A traditional story which has been handed down from the past, often by word of mouth, but also in writing.

Pilgrimage A journey which people make to a holy place as a way of showing their beliefs.

Resurrection Rising from the dead to live again. This is the name which Christians have given to the time when they believe that Jesus rose from his grave after he had been crucified.

Regatta A gathering, or meeting, of boats in order to have a race or other boat competition.

Sacrifice Something which people give to a god or spirit. Often it is a gift of an animal or of food.

Traditions Beliefs, customs and ideas which have been passed on from one generation of people to the next, for example from grandparents to parents, and from parents to children.

BOOKS TO READ
Ramadan, Id ul Fitr, Christmas These are three books on festivals from an excellent series which describes the various festivals against the background of their religion, history and legend. There are also suggestions for things to do, to help you find out more and explore the ideas and customs behind the festivals. They can be obtained from the Religious and Moral Education Press.

Festivals around the World, P. Steele, Macmillan 1983. This book has large photographs of thirty festivals.

Annual Festivals, Rites of Passage. These are charts which show many festivals and customs around the world. They can be obtained from Pictorial Charts, 27 Kirchen Rd., London W13 0UD.

Faith and Festivals by M. Palmer, Ward Lock, 1982, has more festivals also.